Math Game 2

Math Game 2

Copyright © 2005 Sam & Youngjin Singapore Pte, Ltd.

World rights reserved. No part of this publication may be stored in a retrieval system, transmitted, or reproduced in any way, including but not limited to photocopy, photograph, magnetic, or other record, without the prior agreement and written permission of the publisher.

ISBN: 981-05-2239-8

Printed in the Republic of Korea.

Distributed by Publishers Group West.

How to contact us

E-mail: feedback@youngjin.com.sg

Address: Youngjin Singapore Pte, Ltd.
70 Anson Road, #22-04, Apex Tower
Singapore 079905

Telephone: +65-6327-1161
Fax: +65-6327-1151

Manager: Suzie Lee
Production Editor: Cris Lee
Copyeditor: Elisabeth Beller
Proofreaders: Elisabeth Beller, Yonie Overton
Story: Tori Jung
Art: Haley Chung
Color: Winsorblue
Book Designer: Litmus
Cover Designer: Namu & Litmus

Math Game 2

A Journey through Math Land!

sam
Story | Tori Jung
Art | Haley Chung
Color | Winsorblue

Y. kids

To Teachers and Parents

The *Math Game* series is not linked to a specific curriculum for children. It is a supplementary tool to help children learn the principles of mathematics naturally through interesting stories. While enjoying the comics, children will discover interesting and real-life aspects of mathematics. There are no supplemental study pages in the text because the book has been designed in a way that allows children to learn on their own while reading. There is a review section at the end of the book to remind children of what they have learned.

Principles of mathematics are explained thoroughly so that anyone who can read and understand English can understand them. Although this book is intended for third graders or older students, the episodes will be interesting for adults as well.

The storyline is as follows: In *Math Game 1*, children who dislike mathematics speak ill of it. The Evil Math King hears them and is angered. He captures one of the children and then challenges the others to come to

Math Land to try to save their friend. The children soon discover the pathway to Math Land, which opens each time they discover a fact of mathematics used in their daily lives. On arriving at Math Land, the children find that they must pass through a number of gates. In *Math Game 2*, as in *Math Game 1*, each gate is guarded by a master of mathematics who gives out problems the children must solve in order to progress. While passing through each gate, the children get more and more interested in mathematics. Do they finally save their friend? You will find the answer to this question in *Math Game 3*.

Leave this book near children. When they open it, they will discover the world of mathematics!

Math Game 2 contains five episodes that teach about natural numbers, odd and even numbers, fractions, decimals, prime numbers, and addition and subtraction.

Episode 1
Natural Numbers, Odd Numbers, and Even Numbers...8

Episode 2
Fractions I...32

Episode 3
Fractions II...58

Episode 4
Decimals...78

Contents

Episode 5
Prime Numbers I...100

Episode 6
Prime Numbers II...124

Episode 7
Addition and Subtraction (+ -)...144

Academic Pages...192

Finally, the numbers on the third bridge are even numbers, which are written "2n."

Hehehe! How's that? Got it now? Okay, now for the question!

Gasp! The question!

As you can see, the three sets of numbers stretch out infinitely. Which set of numbers will have the most numbers?

What?!

You have five minutes!

I-it's starting again! It's always "just five minutes"!

Look behind you!

Karuri—gari—
sari—sara—
go away—ya—

Ahhh!! The bridge has given out!

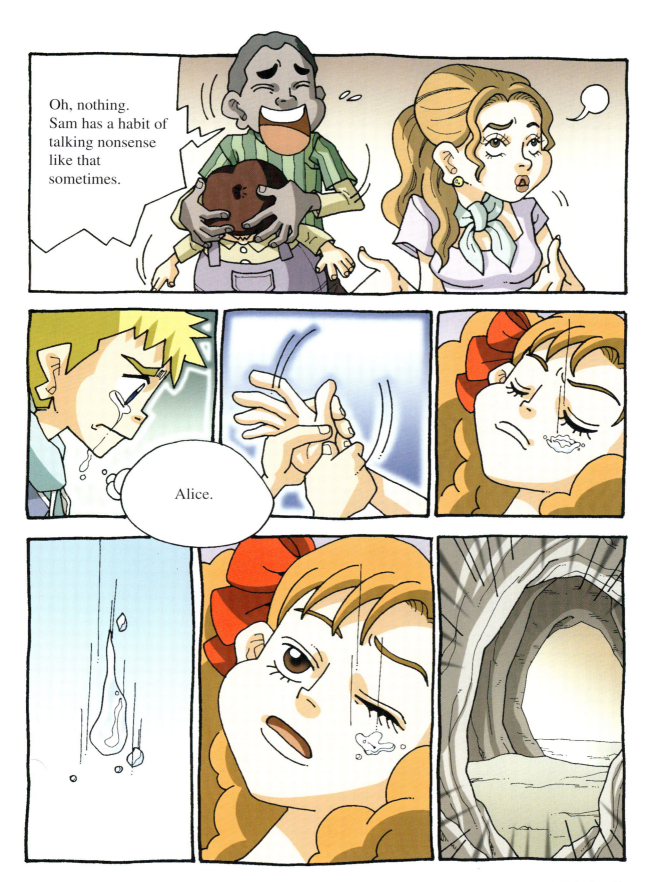

Thank you, everyone. But I'm afraid I have to meet someone for lunch. You guys are going to have to share this cake without me.

What now?

Huh...

Let's see. There are eight of us, so we're going to need eight slices.

Hmmm! How should I cut this?!

Multiply your answer by three.

This is what we call decimals.

What? Decimals?!!

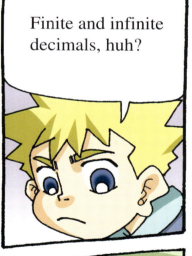

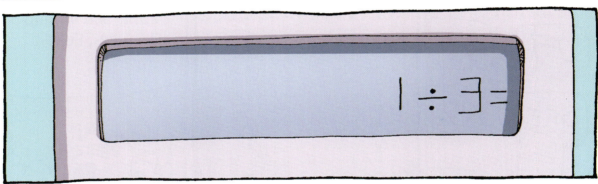

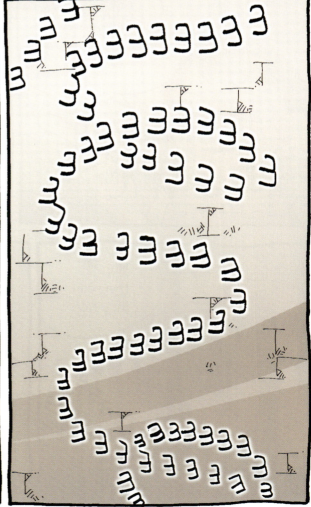

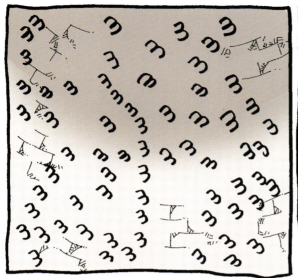

This is ridiculous! How're we supposed to fit all these numbers inside that box?!

Ahhh! There's no right answer! He intends to tickle us to death!!

When I did 1 ÷ 3 the first time, I got 0.33333333333333. But, 1 ÷ 3 is really the fraction, 1/3. So all we have to do is write "1/3" inside that box. Isn't that right?

Yeah! That's it! Why didn't I think of that?!

Yeah! There's no reason to write "0.333333" all the time when we can just write it as "1/3"!!

That's it! That's the right answer!! You've passed the sixth gate!!

Ssssss

Yahoo! We did it!!

Jimmy, you don't look so good these days, and I don't think you're sleeping well. You wake up every morning drenched in sweat.

What's the problem, son.

Is something bothering you, Jimmy?

Huh? No, of course not. There's nothing bothering me.

It's getting harder and harder to pass the gates.

Yeah. That incident on the Nile River still gives me the creeps!

Don't worry! It'll be okay. We've done well so far, haven't we?

Oh yeah!

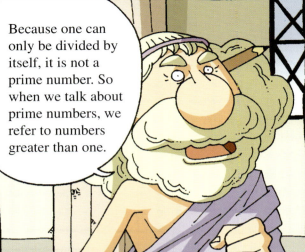

* Gate 3 in *Math Game 1*.

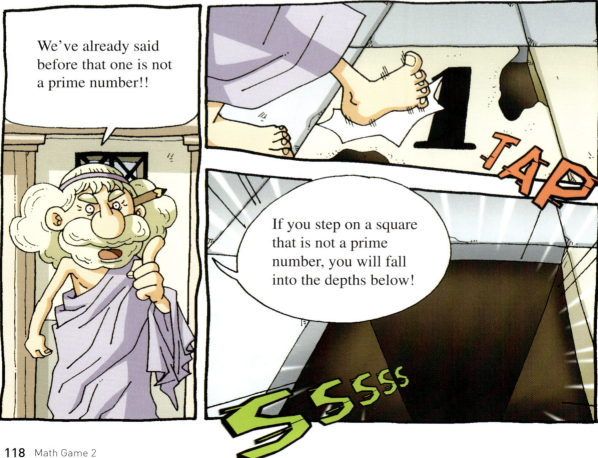

EPISODE 6
Prime Numbers II

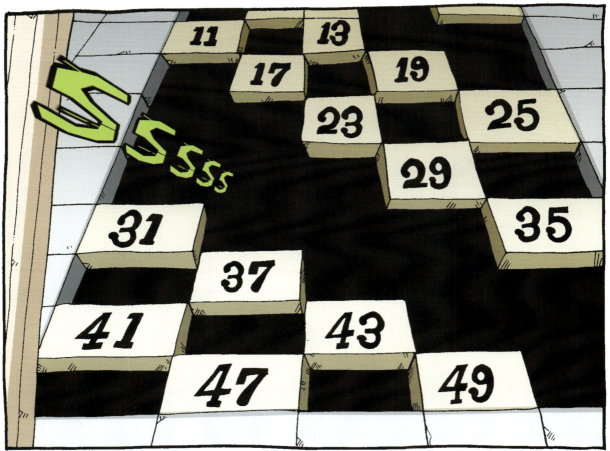

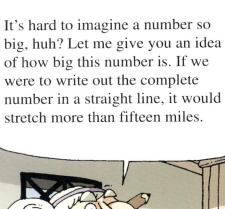

* Eratosthenes was a Greek mathematician. In about 200 BC, he sifted through numbers to discover the prime numbers, and that is why his method is called the "Sieve of Eratosthenes."

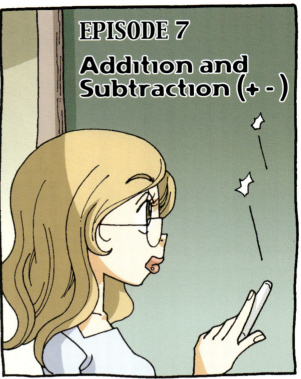

EPISODE 7
Addition and Subtraction (+ -)

352 + 26 =

It's that time again!

What's with the lightening all of a sudden?!

The question for the eighth gate?! What's that?!!

This is the same question I gave my students twenty-three years ago and that is to add up all the numbers from one to one hundred. Back then, Gauss was able to solve the problem in a few seconds. You guys have one minute!!

What———?!

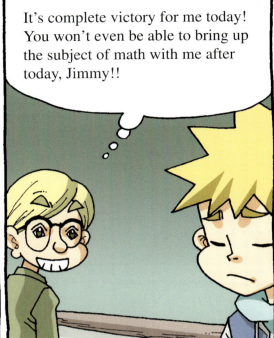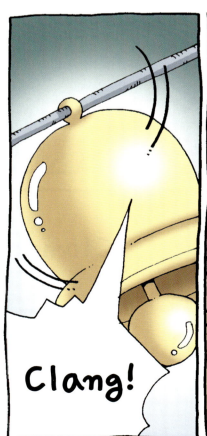

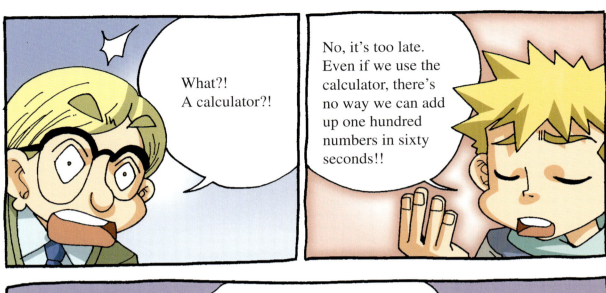

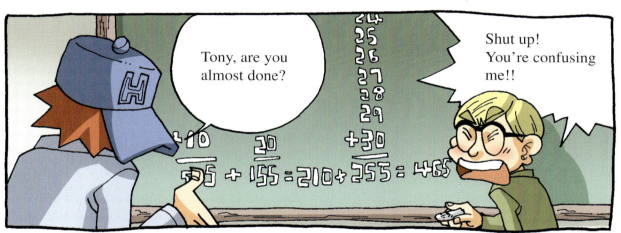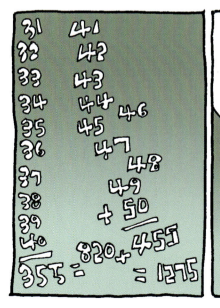

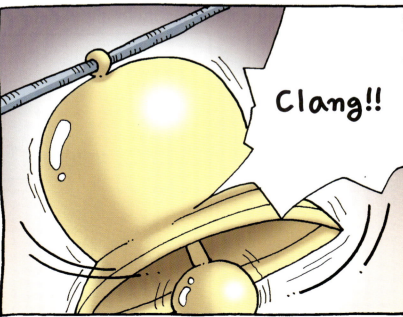

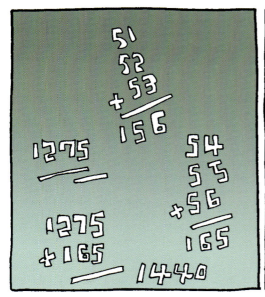

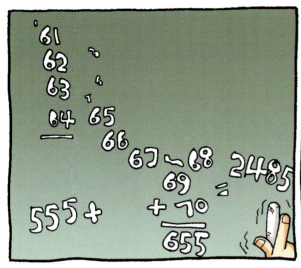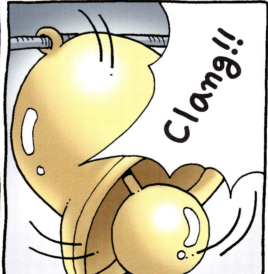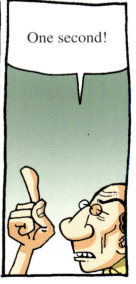

It's the right answer, right?

…

Yes. That's the right answer!

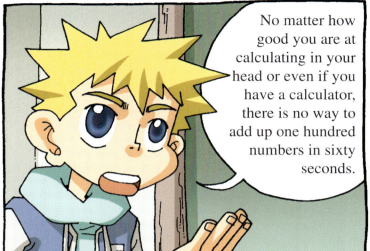

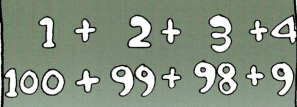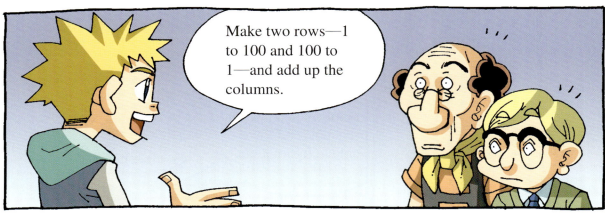

Make two rows—1 to 100 and 100 to 1—and add up the columns.

Okay. The answer for each column is 101, and since there are 100 columns, it's 101×100 or 10,100.

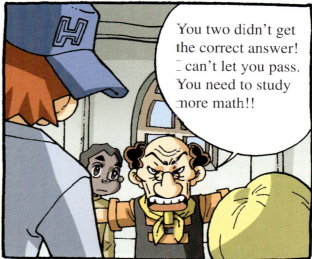

The exciting adventures continue in *Part 3 of Math Game!*

Academic Pages

◎ Fractions

The fractions that we use today originated in Babylonia and were also used in ancient Egypt. It is known that civilizations did very well when they grew up near bodies of water, such as the Nile River in Egypt, the Tigris and Euphrates rivers in Babylonia, the Ganges River in India, and the Yellow River in China. In Egypt, the Nile River flooded very regularly, damaging property, and the ruler needed a way to calculate damage so that taxes could be paid based on the proportion of flood damage each person had suffered. To make this calculation, rulers used fractions.

◎ Decimals

Decimals are very closely related to fractions. Both terms describe numbers that are smaller than one. In order to cut one cake into two equal pieces, we'd cut the cake in half. If we write that as a fraction, each piece is 1/2 of the entire cake. If we write that as a decimal, it looks like "0.5" (which you say out loud as "zero point five"). The point or dot is called a decimal point. Anything to the right of the decimal point is the decimal, meaning it is the part of the number that is less than one.

There are many ways to describe the same number using fractions, equations, or decimals.

Example:
1/10 = 1 ÷ 10 = 0.1
and
1/100 = 1 ÷ 100 = 0.01.

Decimals give us a one way to see the exact value of a number.

◎ Prime Numbers

Any whole number (or "integer") that is larger than the number "1" and that can only be divided by itself and by the number "1" is called a prime number.

According to this definition, 2, 3, 5, 7, 11, 13, 17, 19, 23, and 29 are all prime numbers between 1 and 30. A whole number that is greater than one and that can be divided by a number other than itself or one is called a composite number. Here are some composite numbers: 4 (which can be divided by 2 and 4), 6 (which can be divided by 2, 3, and 6), and 16 (which can be divided by 2, 4, 8, and 16).

The number "1" is neither a prime nor a composite number.

There have been several methods for finding prime numbers. In ancient Roman times, the "Sieve of Eratosthenes" was used to "sift" through numbers to find the primes.

What Is the Sieve of Eratosthenes?

The Sieve of Eratosthenes is a simple step-by-step procedure (or "algorithm") designed by the Greek mathematician and geographer Eratosthenes for finding prime numbers. (Eratosthenes was also famous for being the first to calculate the circumference of the Earth.) To use the Sieve of Eratosthenes to find prime numbers, we first need to list integers in numerical order starting with two. We leave the primes we already know about, such as two and three, but we erase the multiples of those prime numbers. In other words, we erase all the multiples of two from the list except for two itself. If we continue to do this, we'll "sift" through the list until we are left with the numbers that are prime (that is, that can be evenly divided only by themselves and by 1). This method can be used for very long lists of numbers, but if you apply it just to the first twenty integers, you can see that the prime numbers are 2, 3, 5, 7, 11, 13, 17, and 19.

You can use the Sieve of Eratosthenes to find all the prime numbers between one and fifty. First, list all the numbers from one to fifty. Since the number "1" is not a prime number, you can erase it. Then, leaving the number "2" alone, you can erase from the list all the multiples of two. Then do the same for the number "3" and then for "5."

It has been reported that Dr. Martin Nowak of Germany discovered a 7,816,230-digit prime number as part of the GIMPS project.

The GIMPS project was designed to find the largest prime number in the world. In this project, international computer users were asked to contribute their machines fot the experiment with the idea of creating one big supercomputer to find the largest prime number ever.

George Woltman, who first started the GIMPS project, said, "The GIMPS project is an excellent way to learn math, and more volunteers are welcome." The GIMPS project is already underway to find a 10-million-digit prime number.

◎ Adding, Subtracting, Multiplying, and Dividing

The study of mathematics was well developed in ancient Egypt, Mesopotamia (Babylonia), and China. In the farming regions of Egypt and Mesopotamia, math was being used in daily life as early as 2500–2600 BC.

The Egyptians used a type of mathematical system called a decimal system, possibly based on our ten fingers.

The word "calculus," meaning "a method of counting" in English, originally meant "small stone," which suggests that our ancestors used small stones to count. In any case, such simple methods of counting have their problems, and this is probably what gave rise to the mathematical operations of addition (+), subtraction (−), multiplication (×), and division (÷).

1. Addition

Addition is the method used to combine one number or quantity with another number or quantity. Addition is a basic operation, symbolized by placing "+" between two elements, for example, a and b. Addition looks like this: $a + b = c$. The result "c" is called a "sum." The elements "a" and "b" are called "addends."

2. Subtraction

Subtraction is another basic mathematical operation. In subtraction, a number or quantity is taken away from another number or quantity. Subtraction looks like this: $a - b = c$. The result "c" is called the "difference." The element "a" is the "subtractor," and "b" is the "subtrahend."

Subtraction is the opposite of addition.

3. Multiplication

Multiplication is another basic mathematical operation. You can think of it as a series of additions.

In other words, adding three fives together gives us fifteen, but instead of writing this as 5 + 5 + 5 = 15, we can simply write it as 5 × 3 = 15, where 5 and 3 are "multipliers," and 15 is the "product."

4. Division

Division is another basic mathematical operation. It is the opposite of multiplication, and it tells us how many times a number is contained in another number. Division looks like this—a ÷ b = c—where "a" is the "dividend," "b" is the "divisor," and "c" is the result, called the "quotient."

Memo

Memo